Overcoming Depression

Hidden Secrets On How To Combat

Depression

James J. Riley

Table of Contents

OVERCOMING DEPRESSION 1

INTRODUCTION 6

CHAPTER 1.. 8

HIV and Depression.. 8

What exactly are the Symptoms?........................... 11

How could it be Diagnosed? 13

What Can Cause Depression In Hiv Patients?....... 16

How could it be Treated? 18

Depression Medications.. 21

Types of Antidepressants (Set of Medications) 22

CHAPTER 2.. 27

Depression in Men 27

Symptoms of Main Depressive Disorder............... 28

Suicide Risk 29

CHAPTER 3.. 35

Chronic Pain and Depression...................................... 35

Treatment Options... 39

CHAPTER 4.. 42

Separation Anxiety in Kids: How exactly to Help your

son or daughter with Separation Panic 42

Symptoms of Separation PANIC: 44

Treatment of Separation PANIC 46

How parents might help children at home 49

CHAPTER 5.. 52

Teen Depression: The Professionals And Cons Of

Medication.. 52

Risk Factors.. 53

Common antidepressant medications 54

CHAPTER 6.. 60

Male Depression and Stress in Athletes..................... 60

Recognizing the Symptoms 64

How exactly to Help a Man Or Friend with Depression

.... 66

What's the Connection? 70

Bacteria on the mind 71

Your Skill 72

A c k n o w l e d g m e n t s 78

INTRODUCTION

Depression is a state of mind disorder that has something to do with persistent and extreme feeling of sadness, low state of mind, and loss of curiosity. It is with the capacity of causing you to feel worthless. The condition produces negative effects on how you think, take action, and experience - your response to our life generally. It generally makes actions that you loved participating in become uninteresting. That is a fairly common psychological disorder.

In case you are currently battling it, understand that you have people involve in this also. Millions of individuals are struggling from this problem across the globe. It is the most typical illness in the globe, based on the World Health Organization (WHO). It affects nearly 350 million people world-wide.

Overcoming depression is made on this effective,

insightful assumption. Its methods offer fast, effectual relief from major depression by guiding you to create positive and rewarding adjustments in your daily life. This simple, profound procedure reconnects you to the normally occurring benefits of a well-lived existence, which are effective antidotes to emotions of depression. Overcoming Depression can offer recovery and freedom for an incredible number of people who suffer silently from depression.

CHAPTER 1

HIV and Depression

When you check positive for HIV, all of your world can change immediately. From who you show, to selecting your healthcare companies, to monitoring your disease fighting capability, and determining how you would like to cope with HIV in your daily life. There has been a lot more than 700,000 reported cases of Supports America since 1981 and a lot more than 900,000 Americans may presently be contaminated with HIV. It really secure to say that people possess an epidemic on our hands, that's most quickly growing in the feminine and minority populations. It just makes sense to understand that the disease's unwanted effects and how they are able to affect yourself. Much like any diagnosis, numerous side effects may appear simultaneously together with your

HIV contamination. This list isn't exhaustive, but range from:

- Fatigue

- Anemia

- Digestive Problems

- Gas and Bloating

- Diarrhea

- Lipodystrophy (body form changes)

- High levels of fat and sugars in the blood

- Skin Complications (e.g., rashes, dried out skin, hair thinning)

- Peripheral Neuropathy

- Mitochondrial Toxicity

- Osteoporosis

- Osteonecrosis (bone death)

- Depression

Clinical depression may be the most commonly noticed mental health disorder among those identified as having HIV, affecting 22% of the populace. If you have problems with substance abuse as well, this rate could be higher. Common feelings after being identified as having HIV are sadness and grief, but sadness and grief that morph into full-blown clinical depression aren't considered normal responses. Depressive disorder can negatively affect your mind, feeling, body, and behavior. And it frequently go undiagnosed and untreated in those people contaminated with HIV. But, the good thing is, just as there were significant medical developments helping HIV-positive people live fuller, more effective lives, depression remedies help individuals better manage both illnesses. These treatments can boost both survival prices and standard of living in individuals experiencing both HIV and unhappiness.

What exactly are the Symptoms?

When you have been diagnosed to be infected with HIV, you should routinely be choosing medical appointments to best control the infection. Furthermore to physical assessments and examinations, your physician and/or clinician also needs to end up being conducting an annual mental wellness assessment. Because emotions of depression generally co-occur with an analysis of HIV, many sufferers may not instantly seek treatment, considering the fact that it's a normal side-effect of their diagnosis. Likewise, many clinicians neglect to screen efficiently for depression in order not to insult the individual. However, the next symptoms can be due to depression in HIV-positive individuals and should be on your own radar:

- Overall depressed mood

- Lack of interest or pleasure

- Suicidal thoughts

- Feelings of guilt

- Appetite and weight changes

- Sleep disturbance

- Attention and concentration problems

- Changes in vitality and fatigue

- Psychomotor disturbance

- Severe hopelessness or negativism

- Persistent agitation

- Pronounced affective instability

- Maladaptive social functioning

- Feeling slow and sluggish

- Decreased sex drive

How could it be Diagnosed?

While mentioned previously, your physician or clinician ought to be conducting regular mental wellness assessments to determine if you're experiencing any underlying mental disturbances co-occurring together with your HIV illness. After ruling out any physical symptoms, your medical wellness provider should conduct basic screening techniques which have been shown to work in detecting unrecognized depressive disorder. Two simple queries have been demonstrated to have great performance in recognizing major depression in patients:

In the past month, perhaps you have often been bothered by sense down, depressed, or hopeless?

In the past month, perhaps you have often been bothered by small interest or satisfaction in doing things?

If you trust either or both questions, you need to be asked a number of additional questions to help expand help in analysis. Some follow-up queries your medical care supplier may ask you consist of:

Are you having difficulty concentrating? Can you adhere to the plot of a Television show or a publication? Could it be harder than typical to make decisions?

When individuals are ill and feeling depressed, they often times want to just "obtain it around with." Perhaps you have felt that way? Perhaps you have considered killing yourself?

You look just a little jumpy/slow; are you feeling even more restless/moving more gradually than usual? Has other people noticed this?

I observe that you've lost/gained excess weight. Are you feeling even more/less hungry, consuming even more/less than usual? are you blaming yourself for points you haven't any control over?

Are you having difficulty enjoying sex?

Are you fighting together with your spouse or family?

Certain behavioral changes can also be indicative a person identified as having HIV is also experiencing depression. Your clinician should focus on the following adjustments in your behavior that also may help them pinpoint a depressive disorder diagnosis:

- Unexplained medical issues, such as for example pain or fatigue

- Changes in treatment adherence

- A change in functioning to add things such as for example inability to perform everyday living actions, self-imposed isolation, a begin of drug abuse, or a go back to substance abuse

- Inability to create life choices linked to health care and HIV infection treatments

- Becoming preoccupied with particular complications - these problems tend to be minor compared to other complications in your life

- Interpersonal problems

- Showing of challenging behaviors in medical settings

What Can Cause Depression In Hiv Patients?

This may appear to be an apparent question. However, HIV disease itself will not cause melancholy, nor will the progression of the condition automatically result in depression. Critical "crisis factors" are normal "entry" factors of a depressive condition in HIV-infected people. These common crisis factors include:

- Initial HIV diagnosis

- Telling family and friends you have been

HIV-infected

- New medication introductions

- Acknowledgement of new symptoms and disease progression awareness

- Hospitalization

- Physical illness

- Death of a substantial other

- AIDS diagnosis

- A go back to a higher-level of working (e.g., heading back to work, heading back to school)

- Main life changes (e.g., birth, relocation, modification of jobs, lack of a job, being pregnant, end of a romantic relationship)

- Making end-of-life and long term planning decisions

How could it be Treated?

Depression treatment is crucial in patients identified as having HIV. If the patient remain untreated, depression could cause HIV-infected individuals to avoid their treatments, stop medical appointments, and also to actively not really stay involved in personal care generally. Furthermore, not treating despair can result in more dangerous behavior, including alcohol misuse, drug use, and getting careless in behaviors that may infect others with HIV. Furthermore to producing your HIV disease improvement quicker than normal, unhappiness can lead to loss of life by suicide and an over-all poor of life.

The good thing is there are treatment plans available to assist you to cope together with your depression, which can improve your HIV prognosis as well. Lifestyle changes and medicines have got both been effective equipment in helping people that have HIV fight depression.

Antidepressant medications have already been proven effective equipment in the treating depression. In case you are on antidepressants and so are also dealing with HIV, absorb any unwanted effects while on these medicines. This is because of possible interactions between your antidepressants and other medicines you are acquiring for your HIV infections. The most commonly recommended antidepressants are Selective Serotonin Reuptake Inhibitors (SSRIs) and tricyclic's antidepressants. Both could cause side results, such as for example loss of libido and function, headaches, insomnia, exhaustion, erratic heartbeat, constipation, and upset stomach. All medicines should be used under a doctor's care.

Certain lifestyle changes are also found to work in treating depression if you have been identified as having HIV. These consist of regular exercise and contact with sunlight, counseling, stress administration, and improved sleeping practices. Massage and acupuncture are also found nearly as good alternative therapies to depressive disorder.

To obtain the most away of your treatments:

- Head to routine medical checkups

- Don't stop acquiring your HIV or depression medications (unless encouraged by a health care provider)

- Learn all you can easily about both of your conditions - HIV and major depression - and learn indicators and symptoms

- Avoid alcohol and drugs

- Regularly attend counseling sessions

- Stay active

Depression Medications

A closer look at medicine for depression and choosing the best treatment for you. Medication can be a highly effective intervention for treating the symptoms of depressive disorder. Not absolutely all antidepressants, however, function the same manner. The antidepressant your physician will prescribe for you frequently depends on your unique symptoms of major depression, potential unwanted effects, and other factors.

Most antidepressants function by affecting chemical substances in the brain referred to as neurotransmitters.

The neurotransmitters serotonin, norepinephrine, and dopamine are connected with depression. How medicines impact these neurotransmitters determines the course of antidepressants to that they belong.

Types of Antidepressants (Set of Medications)

Selective serotonin reuptake inhibitors (SSRIs) - SSRIs will be the most commonly approved kind of antidepressants. They affect serotonin in the mind, and they're more likely to possess fewer side effects for many people. SSRIs range from citalopram (Celexa), escitalopram (Lexapro), fluoxetine (Prozac), paroxetine (Paxil), and sertraline (Zoloft).

Serotonin and norepinephrine reuptake inhibitors (SNRIs) - SNRIs will be the second most commonly recommended kind of antidepressants. SNRIs range from duloxetine (Cymbalta), desvenlafaxine (Pristiq), levomilnacipran (Fetzima), and venlafaxine (Effexor).

Norepinephrine- dopamine reuptake inhibitors (NDRIs) - Bupropion (Wellbutrin) may be the most generally prescribed type of NDRI. It offers fewer unwanted effects than any other antidepressants and may also be used to take care of anxiety.

Tricyclic antidepressants - Tricyclics are recognized for causing more unwanted effects than other styles of antidepressants, so they are unlikely to be recommended unless various other medications are ineffective. For example amitriptyline (Elavil), desipramine (Norpramin), doxepin (Sinequan), imipramine (Tofranil), nortriptyline (Pamelor), and protriptyline (Vivactil).

Monoamine oxidase inhibitors (MAOIs) - MAOIs have significantly more serious side effects, thus they are rarely recommended unless other medications usually do not function. MAOIs have many conversation results with foods and other medications, so individuals who take them may need to change their diet plan and other medicines. SSRIs and several other medicines taken for mental disease can't be taken with MAOIs.

Additional antidepressants that don't match a category are referred to as atypical antidepressants.

Speaking with Your Doctor

It is necessary to communicate regularly together with your doctor if you are taking an antidepressant, particularly if you are recommended any various other medications. Keep an eye on your symptoms to ensure that they can find a very good medication for your melancholy, and also keep an eye on any side results you have. If you're having difficulty finding a medicine that functions, drug-genetic testing might help your physician determine appropriate options. Should incase where you are pregnant or breastfeeding, make sure to inquire what medicine is safest.

Some antidepressants carry warnings that they could increase suicidal thoughts, particularly among teenagers. Be sure to talk to your doctor in the event that you encounter any suicidal thoughts while on the medicine or monitor your son or daughter if they're taking an antidepressant.

Above all, it's vital that you are not discouraged if an

antidepressant did not properly fit for you personally. With persistence, observation, and conversation, you as well as your doctor will get the medication that greatest suits your symptoms and requirements.

CHAPTER 2

Depression in Men

Everyone feels sad, irritable, or tired sometimes. Many people experience problems sleeping when they're under tension. Their normal reactions awaken stressors that typically move in a few days.

Major depressive disorder differs. Though insomnia and exhaustion tend to be the presenting problems, people who have depression experience depressed disposition or lack of interest in regular day to day activities for weeks at the same time.

The 12-month prevalence of main depressive disorder is approximately 7%. Although women knowledge experiences higher rates of depressive disorder (1.5-3-fold higher) from early adolescence, men do experience depression.

Symptoms of Main Depressive Disorder

The fundamental feature of main depressive disorder is an interval of two weeks where there is usually either depressed mood the majority of the day almost every day or lack of interest or satisfaction in almost all activities. Various other potential medical indications include:

Significant weight loss, dieting or weight gain and changes in appetite

Insomnia or hypersomnia almost every day

Psychomotor agitation or retardation (a clinical term for a condition that describes activities that have zero purpose such as for example tapping fingertips or toes; pacing an area, etc.) nearly each day

Fatigue or lack of energy almost every day

Emotions of worthlessness or excessive guilt

Impaired capability to think or focus, and/or indecisiveness

Recurrent thoughts of death, recurrent suicidal ideation without a plan, or a suicide attempt or suicide plan

The symptoms of main depressive disorder cause significant distress or impairment in social, occupational, or the areas of functioning.

Suicide Risk

The probability of suicidal behavior exists all the time during a main depressive episode. The many consistent risk element is a past background of efforts or threats, but it's vital that you remember that many completed suicides aren't preceded by unsuccessful suicides. Although women with major depression will attempt suicide, men will die by suicide

Symptoms of melancholy in men

Differing people experience different symptoms of depression, and symptoms for men may vary from symptoms for women. Men or even more likely to feel extremely tired and irritable, weary in work, family members, and/or hobbies, and also have difficulty sleeping.

Men will probably exhibit a few of the following symptoms of despair:

- Experience sad or "empty"

- Sense irritable, angry, hopeless, or anxious

- Lack of interest in work, family members, or additional hobbies or passions (including sex)

- Feeling very tired

- Difficulty concentrating

- Sleep disturbance (struggling to rest or sleeping)

- Changes in diet plan (overeating or not wanting to

eat at all)

- Thoughts of suicide, suicide attempts

- Somatic complaints (aches or pains, headaches, digestive problems)

- Inability to meet up daily responsibilities.

Treatment

A combination of medicine and psychotherapy works well for many people with depression. Lifestyle changes can also help.

Lifestyle

In moderate cases of depression, daily exercise improved diet plan, and a particular sleep routine can help in alleviating some symptoms.

Psychotherapy

Psychotherapy, or "chat therapy," is an over-all term that

identifies treating depression by speaking through your triggers and responses with a certified mental doctor. There are various kinds of psychotherapy which can be effective in treating unhappiness.

Cognitive Behavioral Therapy (CBT): This short-term therapy works to displace unfavorable and unproductive thought patterns with an increase of realistic and useful kinds. This treatment targets taking specific actions to control and reduce symptoms.

Interpersonal "talk" therapy: This attachment-focused therapy centers on resolving interpersonal problems and symptomatic recovery.

Problem-solving therapy: This treatment helps people learn tools to effectively manage the unwanted effects of stressful lifestyle events.

Psychotherapy may help people who have depression:

- Cope with an emergency

- Identify and change negative beliefs

- Explore relationships and encounters and build positive connections

- Find adaptive methods to solve problems

- Identify issues that donate to depression

- Set realistic goals

- Develop the capability to tolerate pressure and distress.

- Medication Management

Either a primary treatment physician or a psychiatrist can help with medication administration. Selective serotonin reuptake inhibitor (SSRI) and serotonin-norepinephrine reuptake inhibitor (SNRI) medicines are both effective remedies for depression. Other feasible medications consist of norepinephrine-dopamine reuptake inhibitors (NDRI), atypical antidepressants, tricyclic antidepressants, and monoamine oxidase inhibitors

(MAOI).

Differing people have different responses to medications. It's vital that you work closely together with your primary treatment doctor or psychiatrist and state any side effects. By no means stop taking antidepressant medicine without consulting the prescribing doctor. Stopping treatment abruptly can create withdrawal-like symptoms and result in an unexpected worsening of depressive symptoms.

Hospitalization

Severe instances of depression may require hospitalization. Psychiatric treatment in a medical center setting helps patients remain safe until their feeling improves, particularly regarding suicidal thoughts or suicide tries.

CHAPTER 3

Chronic Pain and Depression

Chronic pain is usually a term utilized to spell out pain that lasts beyond the normal time it requires for a sickness or problems to heal. Sometimes chronic discomfort is also referred to as discomfort that lasts much longer than 90 days. Research suggests that from 30 to 50% of individuals with chronic discomfort also have a problem with depression or anxiety.

Chronic pain isn't only a physical condition-it's a psychological one as well which has tremendous influence more than a person's thoughts and moods. People who have chronic discomfort may isolate from others or struggle to achieve flexibility they once experienced. Chronic discomfort isn't just connected with physical accidental injuries either, as it could stem from circumstances like cardiovascular disease, arthritis, migraines, or diabetes.

Sometimes it could be difficult to evaluate whether chronic pain offers led to depressive disorder, or vice versa. People who have chronic pain are three times more likely to build up symptoms of major depression or anxiety, and folks with depression are three times as more likely to develop persistent discomfort. Depression frequently could cause unexplained discomfort, such as for example headaches or back discomfort, and folks who are depressed might battle to improve or maintain physical wellness. Subsequently, chronic pain can result in sleep problems, increased stress, or emotions of guilt or worthlessness connected with melancholy. These influences can create a routine that's hard to break.

Although depression can also debilitate people who have chronic pain, these folks may be less inclined to recognize and discuss symptoms of depression with their doctor. Actually, half of most depressed persons who go to the doctor just complain about physical symptoms. Because both discomfort and depression make one another difficult to take care of, it's vital that you address both when analyzing treatment options.

You might be experiencing depression furthermore to chronic pain in case you have a few of the following symptoms:

- insufficient interest in activities

- depressed mood or irritability

- changes in sleep patterns

- changes in appetite

- emotions of guilt or despair

- lack of energy

- trouble concentrating

- Suicidal thoughts.

- Assembling cure Team

Patients advantage the most when chronic discomfort and depressive disorder are treated together and use a team of individuals. This team of specialists may include:

Physician: A doctor can offer a thorough exam and evaluation, provide a diagnosis, and, if required, prescribe both discomfort and psychiatric medications.

Pain specialist: A discomfort specialist can educate the individual about the partnership between chronic discomfort and despair and help design cure plan.

A Therapist: Regular classes with a therapist been trained in cognitive behavioral therapy, or various other form of psychotherapy, might help address anxious or bad thinking patterns and train coping skills that decrease symptoms of both discomfort and depression. They are able to also use patients' families to greatly help them better understand chronic discomfort and depression.

A Physical Therapist: A physical therapist who might help improve mobility, decrease pain, and increase low disposition by introducing useful exercises and muscle rest techniques.

Other experts such as for example nutritionists, acupuncturists, and occupational therapists can offer special knowledge to greatly help curb chronic discomfort and depression.

Treatment Options

There are many treatment plans which can offer relief and healing to chronic pain and depression. A few of these include:

Talk therapy - Also called psychotherapy, talk therapy might help an individual modification patterns in thinking, find out coping abilities for symptoms, and assist in preventing future depressive symptoms.

Stress-reduction skills - These abilities range from exercise, muscle rest, meditation, positive thinking, etc. Therapists, pain professionals, physical therapists and others can offer recommendations to match the needs and passions of the patient.

Medication - Regular analgesics and antidepressant medicines may be prescribed to greatly help fight symptoms. For extreme discomfort, opioids could be prescribed, but speak to your doctor about the dangers and any background of substance make use of first.

Peer support - Many people discover that organizations for chronic discomfort, mental illness, or both can offer both psychological support and psycho-education. If there isn't any personal group in your town, consider looking on-line for support.

Inpatient or outpatient discomfort programs - More intensive applications can offer immediate and long-term support when depression and/or chronic discomfort is severe. These applications typically offer onsite medical support, specific and group therapy, and psycho-education for reducing tension and pain.

If you think that you may have depression furthermore to chronic pain, by no means hesitate in all honesty together with your doctor about the emotional and also physical symptoms you are experiencing. Because discomfort is invisible doesn't imply that it isn't actual or that it can't end up being treated. Consider today who you can recruit to assist you regain control over the body, mind, and spirit.

CHAPTER 4

Separation Anxiety in Kids: How exactly to Help your son or daughter with Separation Panic

What "separation anxiety" tend to be used through the early toddler years? As toddlers are more alert to their surroundings and start to understand the globe around them, they battle with individual from caregivers. A toddler who once transitioned to a nanny or daycare establishing easily screams and cries when the caregiver leaves. Though problematic for the caregiver to witness, this component of childhood advancement is rather common and there are methods to ease these transitions.

What parents aren't usually prepared for may be the comeback of separation anxiety in "big children." Both school-age kids and adolescents can have a problem with separation stress and, in some instances, it can lead to Separation PANIC. Based on the Diagnostic and Statistical Manual of Mental Disorders, Separation PANIC sometimes appears in 4% of kids and 1.6% of adolescents, which makes it the most prevalent panic among children beneath the age of 12.

While a couple of tears at fall off and after college meltdowns are pretty common among children and really should not raise warning flag, symptoms of Separation PANIC certainly are a cause for concern. College refusal, rest disturbance, and excessive distress when confronted with separation can negatively influence a child's day-to-day time living.

Symptoms of Separation PANIC:

The defining feature of Separation PANIC is excessive fear or anxiety regarding the separation from your home or attachment figures. This dread or anxiety exceeds what's to be likely of the individual provided his/her developmental level.

Kids and adolescents with Separation PANIC experience at least 3 of the next symptoms:

- Recurrent extreme distress when anticipating or experiencing separation from your home or attachment numbers (parents or additional caregivers)

- Persistent and excessive be concerned on the subject of losing an attachment physique or possible injury to them by illness, incident, disasters, or death

- Persistent worry on the subject of experiencing an urgent separation from an attachment number (kidnapping, accident, growing to be ill)

- Refusal to venture out or abroad, including to college or alternative activities, due to concern with separation

- Excessive concern with being only or without attachment figures

- Refusal to sleep abroad or fall asleep without having to be near an attachment figure

- Nightmares about separation

- Physical complaints including headaches, stomachaches, and/or vomiting when from attachment figures

Symptoms of Separation PANIC in kids and adolescents last for in least a month and trigger significant distress.

College refusal is normal with kids and adolescents fighting the disorder and may result in poor college attendance and poor educational functioning. Separation PANIC may also impair social associations and family relationships.

Children with Separation PANIC have a tendency to shadow parents throughout the house, have a problem playing or being only, and have difficulty in bedtime. They often need a mother or father or caregiver to remain with them if they drift off and make their method in to the parents' bedroom if they wake at night time.

Treatment of Separation PANIC

There are many commonly used treatments for Separation PANIC. With kids and adolescents, the earlier you intervene and look for specialized help, the most likely your child will encounter a positive treatment end result.

Finding a psychotherapist who also specializes in kids and adolescents may be the first rung on the ladder toward helping your son or daughter cope. There are various kinds of psychotherapy which can be effective in dealing with Separation Anxiety Disorder.

Cognitive Behavioral Therapy (CBT):

This is actually the primary kind of psychotherapy recommended for treatment of Separation PANIC. Through CBT, children figure out how to identify their anxious emotions and their physical responses to anxious thoughts. They figure out how to determine their triggers and the idea patterns that donate to their anxious emotions. Through a number of techniques, kids learn ways of manage their anxious thoughts and emotions and cope with their feelings.

Family therapy:

Incorporating parents and various other family members in to the treatment process can easily improve outcomes for the kid. In family member's therapy, parents and siblings can find out new methods to interact with the kid and tease out patterns of behavior. They are able to also learn useful ways of help the kid when anxiety spikes.

Play therapy:

Younger children may have a problem connecting the dots between thoughts, feelings, and activities. For these kids, play therapy might help them demonstrate and procedure their emotions and figure out how to cope with them.

Relaxation training is vital for kids and adolescents fighting Separation Anxiety Disorder. Yoga breathing, guided rest, and progressive muscle rest can also help kids and adolescents figure out how to self-soothe during anxious occasions.

Some children and adolescents continue steadily to have a problem with symptoms of Separation PANIC even during treatment. If symptoms continue steadily to negatively affect your son or daughter and make it problematic for your child to wait for school or even go out, medication will help. It's vital that you seek a medicine evaluation from a kid and adolescent psychiatrist, as medicines can have significant unwanted effects for children.

How parents might help children at home

There are things parents can do to greatly help children and adolescents figure out how to manage their anxious feelings. Parent support plays an integral role in assisting kids figure out how to cope individually. Try these strategies in the home to help your son or daughter be successful outside of the house:

- Make a program to help your son or daughter transition to school each morning (arrive early, become the teacher's helper prior to the other kids appear, get some exercise upon the playground prior to the bell rings)

- Help your son or daughter reframe anxious thoughts simply by creating a set of positive thoughts (it even really helps to write these upon cards and place them in the backpack)

- Write daily lunchbox notes that include positive phrases

- Avoid overscheduling. Concentrate on playtime, downtime, and healthful sleep habits

- Alert your son or daughter to changes in program ahead of time

- Empathize with your kid and touch upon progress

made

CHAPTER 5

Teen Depression: The Professionals And Cons Of Medication

If your child is fighting depression, you may be wondering if medicine might help. Antidepressant medicines, while generally secure, can have unpleasant unwanted effects, and latest warnings about teenagers and antidepressant make use of are worrisome. On the other hand, they can also significantly improve your mood. Therefore, it's vital that you weigh the professionals and cons of medicine use.

Teen depression is a significant mental health condition that triggers persistent emotions of sadness and lack of interest in activities. It impacts what sort of teen thinks and behaves and will negatively impact school, family members, and social functioning.

Based on the National Institute of Mental Wellness, around 3 million American adolescents, age group 12 to 17, got at least one main depressive episode in 2015. This quantity represented 12.5% of the adolescent population.

Risk Factors

Research displays the strongest risk elements for unhappiness in adolescence certainly are a genealogy of depression and contact with psychosocial stress. Other things to consider consist of developmental factors, hormone changes, and psychosocial adversity.

Other factors that may trigger teen depression include:

- Bullying and additional peer issues

- Academic pressure or problems

- Chronic disease

- Alcohol or drug use

- Family discord

- Sleep deprivation

- Confusion about sexual orientation

- Other mental health disorders

- Learning disabilities and ADHD

- Low self-esteem

- Background of violence (witness to or victim of)

Common antidepressant medications

There are many different types of antidepressant medications. Each functions to change what sort of brain procedures the neurotransmitters that have an effect on moods and feelings. Serotonin, dopamine, and norepinephrine are several brain chemical substances that regulate our feelings and energy levels.

Selective serotonin reuptake inhibitors (SSRIs): When taken as directed and less than close medical supervision, SSRIs might help teens manage symptoms of depression with hardly any unwanted effects. SSRIs elevate feeling by raising serotonin.

Monoamine oxidase inhibitors (MAOIs): They were some of the 1st antidepressants developed. MAOIs boost serotonin by blocking the enzyme that breaks it down. MAOIs aren't prescribed as much because they are able to have serious unwanted effects and drug or meals interactions.

Tricyclic antidepressants (TCAs): These antidepressants aren't commonly recommended for teens or more youthful patients due to part effects unless the individual is usually unresponsive to SSRIs.

Atypical antidepressants: These antidepressants (including Well butyrin, Cymbalta, and Effexor) have fewer unwanted effects and tend to be better tolerated by young patients.

Pros of medication

For most teens, antidepressants coupled with psychotherapy are a highly effective way to take care of depression. Antidepressants might help teens in the next ways:

- Improve mood

- Improve appetite

- Increased focus

- Resolve sleep disturbance connected with depression

- Lower anxious symptoms that may occur with depression

- Lower depressive symptoms that may trigger suicidal thoughts

- It must be noted that the chance of suicide occurs all the time throughout a major depressive show, and teens ought to be carefully monitored and evaluated during this time period.

Antidepressants function best in mixture with psychotherapy (including procedure oriented therapy or cognitive behavioral therapy). During psychotherapy, teenagers can learn coping abilities to control depression and handle psychosocial stressors. They are able to also explore triggers of depressive disorder and how exactly to mitigate those triggers later on.

Cons of medication

All medications have unwanted effects. Some antidepressants could cause minor unwanted effects that are irritating but manageable, while some can lead to serious unwanted effects. It's vital that you discuss all potential unwanted effects prior to starting treatment with an antidepressant, and maintain a close eye on your own teen (including regular appointment with the prescribing doctor).

SSRIs, the mostly prescribed antidepressants, may have the next side effects:

- Gastrointestinal symptoms

- Insomnia or sedation

- Dry mouth

- Dizziness

- Weight gain

- Headaches

- Sexual side effects

It's important to remember that antidepressants aren't a

"magic pill" for depression, and may take 6-8 weeks to alleviate symptoms.

Another thing to consider is that recent study shows no clear advantage of treatment with antidepressants for kids and adolescents.

The end result is that every teen differs. One teen might encounter benefits and few unwanted effects, while another might acknowledge light relief of depressive symptoms and several unwanted effects. A team method of treating major depression (with or without medicine) may be the best wager for teens.

CHAPTER 6

Male Depression and Stress in Athletes

Michael Phelps, the most decorated athlete in Olympic background with 28 medals, has acknowledged that following the 2012 video games, his longtime depressive disorder was thus overwhelming, he considered killing himself.

"There is one point I didn't wish to be alive," he tells CBS News. "I believe it's a thing that nobody's really discussed previously because we're said to be this big, macho, solid person that has zero weaknesses. You understand, we're said to be perfect."

Starting the Conversation

The swimmer's candid disclosure is among other recent admissions by top athletes of their own mental health struggles. In March, the NBA's Kevin Like wrote an essay about his encounter with anxiety attacks for The Players Tribune and the NFL's Brandon Brooks of the Philadelphia Eagles informed ESPN about his struggles with panic.

Phelps had previously disclosed to US Weekly that he battled melancholy and said he was speaking out about his knowledge to let others find out "if really is OK never to be OK."

"It takes power and lots of guts for these man athletes to intensify and talk about it publicly that they've been struggling. It's incredibly essential that they are performing this," says John Ogrodniczuk, PhD, professor and director of the Psychotherapy System in the Division of Psychiatry at the University of British Columbia. Dr. Ogrodniczuk can be the founder of HeadsUpGuys.org, a site for boys and males devoted to busting despair myths and providing assets and help.

"It can't be underestimated how powerful that seemingly basic take action is for others fighting these difficulties," he says of the top sports athletes speaking out. "I obtain the sense that men need permission from various other guys to say this is okay that they might be having some struggles. This business tend to be held in high respect in society; if it's ok to allow them to perform it, it's okay for me."

Overcoming the Stigma

Ruben C. Gur, PhD, a professor of psychiatry and neurology at the University of Pennsylvania's Perelman College of Medication, concurs, adding a main obstacle in dealing with mental illness may be the stigma that complements it.

"Imagine if there is a stigma like this about

cardiovascular disease or kidney disease," Dr. Gur says. "People could have those symptoms and believe they should hide the symptoms. Unfortunately, this is the scenario with mental disorders. People don't admit it to themselves so when they perform, they try to conceal it, cope with it without looking for professional help."

"There are treatments plus they function," he says. "The issue is people don't arrive to get those remedies."

That stigma-particularly among males-includes the myths that depression is an indicator of weakness; that feeling unfortunate or down isn't manly; and that guys should not request for help and also cope by themselves, relating to Dr. Ogrodniczuk, who studies men and depression.

"Among the prime known reasons for unhappiness in men may be the inability of expressing themselves openly and with emotion," says Henry Montero, MSW of

Alquimedez Mental Wellness Counseling in NEW YORK. "This is why I believe men will use external solutions to cope with the inward turmoil and discomfort due to depression. Men often cope with depressive disorder by over-working; they observe substance abuse (self-medication) as a means out of major depression and anxiousness, outbursts of anger that could result in abusive behavior design on others including their companions," Montero explains.

Recognizing the Symptoms

Men will probably exhibit a few of the following symptoms of melancholy:

- Feeling unfortunate or "empty"

- Sense irritable, angry, hopeless, or anxious

- Lack of interest in work, family members, and also hobbies or passions (including sex)

- Feeling very tired

- Difficulty concentrating

- Sleep disturbance

- Changes in diet plan (overeating or not wanting to eat at all)

- Thoughts of suicide, suicide attempts

- Somatic complaints (aches or pains, headaches, digestive problems)

- Inability to meet up daily responsibilities.

Other potential medical indications include:

- Significant weight loss you should definitely dieting or weight gain and changes in appetite

- Insomnia or hypersomnia almost every day

- Psychomotor agitation nearly each day

- Fatigue or lack of energy almost every day

- Emotions of worthlessness or excessive guilt

- Impaired capability to think or focus, and/or indecisiveness

- Recurrent thoughts of death, recurrent suicidal ideation without a plan, or a suicide attempt or suicide plan

How exactly to Help a Man Or Friend with Depression

To make a healthy culture for men expressing emotions better, they have to feel safe and sound expressing them to begin with. "Crying should not be connected with gender functions. Men (and males) don't cry because they're poor," Montero says, "they cry because crying-like various other emotions-is a standard expression for everyone. Crying is definitely a simple emotion. Its period to improve how society perceives psychological responses in men. This edition of masculinity can be toxic and must quit."

Loved types and friends of males and men are essential in offering help for sufferers. "Whether it's a partner, a pal, a close colleague at the job, the doctor trying to greatly help, fighting any mental wellness challenge is difficult. It's so easier whenever there are people around you to greatly help when you're able to share the responsibility."

For those trying to greatly help, understand that males "aren't naturally inclined to talk." "Mild prodding can sometimes encourage them to reveal what is certainly on their mind, and tell them there is nothing at all to become ashamed of. That is true for just about any disorder. If a youngster doesn't let you know their belly hurts, we won't understand they have trouble with their abdomen. The same holds true with their mental existence."

"In case you are wondering if a man you know could be dealing with despair and you don't quite understand how to begin that conversation, it may be something as simple as saying, 'Hey Joe, how are things?' or 'You don't appear to be your regular self recently, anything up?'"

"You don't need to instantly say, 'I question if you're depressed.' You want to create an open up forum for a discussion to begin with and with that, you are demonstrating you possess an open up and willing to hear. And you intend to help him connect to services."

After voicing observations, as Dr. Ogrodniczuk recommended, it's vital that you be empathic, open-minded, and nonjudgmental in your discussion. For a number of men, it's hard to start judging some other person, so it's essential to tell him that you're available to whatever he must say.

The Gut Mind Connection: How Gut Wellness Affects Mental Health

How will the gut-brain axis impact your mental health? Experts say managing the bacterial populace of the gastrointestinal tract can help improve symptoms of mental disorders

Your micro biome-the varied population of microbes (bacteria) that reside in your gastrointestinal (GI) tract plays an essential role in the fitness of your gut, and also areas of your physical health, from inflammatory pores and skin disorders to obesity. Experts now say that role of promoting great wellness may extend to add to the health of the human brain and neurological systems.

What's the Connection?

The thousands of various kinds of both "good" and "bad" bacteria that populate the micro biome normally exist in a balance and only beneficial bacteria that assist in preventing overgrowth of bad bacteria that may harm your health. Research have demonstrated there is potential damage connected with an imbalance in the micro biome because of swelling, intestinal permeability or insufficient bacterial diversity, some of which may become connected with an overgrowth of harmful bacteria. In some instances, researchers are met with the classic "poultry or egg" query with regards to the association between gut bacteria's and poor health, in conditions of which comes first. Does an overgrowth trigger the disorder or will the disorder trigger an overgrowth of poor bacteria?

Bacteria on the mind

Current thinking in neuro-scientific neuropsychology and the analysis of mental health issues includes solid speculation that bipolar disorder, schizophrenia, and other mental or neurological problems can also be connected with alternations in the micro biome. Experts speculate that any disruption to the standard, healthful balance of bacteria's in the micro biome could cause the disease fighting capability to overreact and donate to irritation of the GI tract, subsequently leading to the advancement of symptoms of disease that happen not only during your body, but also in the human brain.

This technique of connections and communication between your gastrointestinal tract and the mind is known as the "gut-brain axis." Some experts speculate that attacks occurring in early existence could negatively influence the mucosal membrane in the GI tract, disrupting the gut-mind axis, and interfering with regular brain advancement. The mucosal membrane may also be modified in different ways, such as through poor diet options, radiation treatment, antibiotic make use of, and chemotherapy.

Your Skill

To keep up or restore the fitness of your micro biome and support great general health, it is essential to keep up a strong balance and only beneficial bacteria in your digestive system. The first rung on the ladder is to consume a well-balanced diet which includes foods with probiotic or prebiotic things that support microbial wellness by assisting to restore stability to the gut micro biome. They are foods which contain live beneficial (probiotic) bacteria's and, regarding prebiotics, contain chemicals like particular types of fiber that nurture the development of probiotic bacteria.

Probiotic Foods

Until more is well known, look to a number of easily available probiotic foods supplying varying amounts beneficial live bacteria that grow during carefully managed fermentation processes. A few of these are common foods you might already end up being including in diet, while some may seem a little even more exotic, though they are plentiful in supermarkets. Probiotic foods and drinks include natural yogurt, kefir, cottage cheese, new sauerkraut, kimchi, kombucha, apple cider vinegar, and miso. Remember that the probiotic ramifications of these food types are destroyed by cooking food, processing, or preserving at high temperature.

Prebiotic Foods

Unlike probiotic foods, prebiotic foods usually do not contain living organisms. They donate to the fitness of the micro biome because they contain indigestible fibers that ferment in the GI tract, where they are consumed by probiotic bacteria's and changed into other healthful chemicals. Prebiotic foods consist of artichokes, leeks, onions, garlic, chicory, cabbage, asparagus, legumes, and oats.

Commercial Supplements

While probiotic health supplements have been shown to boost symptoms of depressive disorder, anxiety, obsessive-compulsive disorder and various other psychological and neurological circumstances, their use ought to be discussed with your physician or mental doctor. Presently, there are no standardized suggestions because researchers have however to determine which bacterial species or mixture of species, dosages and delivery systems can greatly be of help so as to treat particular symptoms and keep maintaining overall health. It really is still unclear whether solitary strains of probiotic bacteria's are as effectual as mixtures of different strains, and if or how any mixture of bacteria's in a product can hinder other medications or additional areas of health.

Microbial Transplant

Food and products represent the most typical ways probiotics could be sent to the gastrointestinal tract, however they aren't the only method. Another type of treatment presently under investigation is called fecal microbial transplant, which is usually just about what it appears like. In short, feces (stool) from a wholesome individual is definitely transplanted to the bowel of somebody with a chronic condition, with the purpose of repopulating their micro biome with an increase of diverse species of bacteria's and reducing symptoms. This system has been proven to work in dealing with gastrointestinal disorders but research into its worth for psychiatric symptoms are in extremely early stages.

Looking Ahead

Nearly all studies searching at the gut-brain axis and the usage of probiotics to lessen symptoms and occurrence of mental health disorders such as for example bipolar and schizophreniare preliminary, preclinical studies that support the idea but possess yet to demonstrate a complete effect in human beings with mental medical issues. Although early study factors to positive outcomes, bigger population, and human medical studies are essential to determine which individuals can truly reap the benefits of probiotic or "psychobiotic" treatment of mental wellness disorders, and how these remedies can best be employed.

Acknowledgments

The Glory of this book success goes to God Almighty and my beautiful Family, Fans, Readers & well-wishers, Customers and Friends for their endless support and encouragements.